LEVERAGING FINTECH FOR WOMEN ENTREPRENEURS IN INDONESIA, THE PHILIPPINES, AND VIET NAM

JULY 2024

ASIAN DEVELOPMENT BANK

ADB

On the cover: Women-owned micro, small, and medium-sized enterprises face barriers to accessing finance, which fintech lenders can address through alternative data assessments and simplified documentation. However, few fintechs specifically target this segment, suggesting a need for tailored products and increased collaboration to overcome barriers like low digital literacy and awareness. Cover design by Josef Ilumin.

CONTENTS

TABLE AND FIGURES

TABLE

FIGURES

FOREWORD

Digital finance holds transformative potential in advancing financial inclusion, a critical priority for the Asian Development Bank (ADB). By leveraging digital finance, we can benefit underserved groups, including micro, small, and medium-sized enterprises (MSMEs) in general and women-owned MSMEs in particular.

MSMEs remain key contributors to GDP, employment, and income inequality. However, they often face challenges in accessing affordable and suitable finance due to issues related to collateral, financial records, credit histories, financial literacy, and digital security skills. Innovations in mobile technology and fintech solutions can create new opportunities and help close the funding gap for MSMEs by facilitating access to a wide range of financial products, simplifying loan management processes, and integrating basic client support and financial literacy services. Advanced fintech solutions often utilize customers' digital footprints, alternative transaction histories, and data trails to tailor their products for MSMEs.

The fintech sector, expected to generate $1.5 trillion in annual revenue by 2030, is expanding rapidly, with the largest markets in Asia and the Pacific.* This growth presents a significant opportunity to enhance financial inclusion through fintech solutions.

Digital financial inclusion is poised to play a pivotal role in the future of the financial sector, with the private sector at the forefront of this shift. The ADB is committed to supporting digital finance by profiling leading innovators and identifying funding opportunities that promote inclusion. Additionally, ADB provides capital and technical assistance to banks and fintech companies driving this inclusion, thereby creating an enabling environment for innovation.

This study explores the fintech landscape in three countries—Indonesia, the Philippines, and Viet Nam. It highlights how fintech improves access to finance for MSMEs, identifies key issues for women entrepreneurs and business owners, and examines current and emerging fintech business models and enabling technologies. It also showcases how certain fintech companies have successfully integrated features specifically designed to serve women entrepreneurs and business owners. A collaborative effort among various stakeholders is essential to overcome the barriers that MSMEs face in accessing financing through digital means.

ADB hopes this research will uncover opportunities presented by fintech and, in turn, support women entrepreneurs across the region. Through these efforts, we aim to build a more inclusive financial ecosystem that benefits all.

Asif Cheema
Director
Private Sector Financial Institutions
Asian Development Bank

---

* Boston Consulting Group. 2023. *Global Fintech 2023: Reimagining the Future of Finance.* https://www.bcg.com/publications/2023/future-of-fintech-and-banking

ACKNOWLEDGEMENTS

This knowledge product is the result of the collaborative efforts of Asian Development Bank (ADB) staff and consultants. This study was prepared by Savita Shankar under the guidance of Sabine Spohn. Akhil Hemrajani, Apurva Kumar, Arvind Sankaran, and Lisette Cipriano provided useful feedback, suggestions and support.

ABBREVIATIONS

ADB	–	Asian Development Bank
BNLP	–	buy now, pay later
BSP	–	Bangko Sentral ng Pilipinas
CIIP	–	Centre for Impact Investing and Practices
e-wallet	–	electronic wallet
fintech	–	financial technology
fintechs	–	fintech companies
FMCG	–	fast-moving consumer goods
GDP	–	gross domestic product
IFC	–	International Finance Corporation
MSMEs	–	micro, small, and medium-sized enterprises
OECD	–	Organisation for Economic Co-operation and Development
OJK	–	Ororitas Jasa Keuangan (Financial Services Authority)
P2P	–	peer-to-peer
SMEs	–	small and medium-sized enterprises
WMSMEs	–	women-owned micro, small, and medium-sized enterprises

EXECUTIVE SUMMARY

Financial technology (fintech) innovations are increasingly viewed by regulators and development sector actors as part of the solution to addressing financial exclusion in developing countries. There is also recognition that fintech companies (fintechs) have roles that are complementary to traditional banks and that there is substantial scope for collaboration between the two. While banks have access to low-cost and stable funding, their branch-based models do not allow last-mile reach and their credit assessment methodologies are unable to adequately assess the unbanked. By using data trails and technological innovations, fintechs can make credit assessments of segments perceived to be "riskier."

Women-owned micro, small, and medium-sized enterprises (WMSMEs) are an important unbanked segment that can benefit from fintech innovations. Providing hard collateral is the most important barrier that WMSMEs face when accessing finance. Fintech lenders who base their credit assessments on alternate data from e-commerce, invoicing, payments, and mobile phones can enable WMSMEs to overcome this barrier. Moreover, fintechs have much simpler documentation requirements compared to traditional banks, another crucial factor in serving this segment.

The fintech sectors in Indonesia, the Philippines, and Viet Nam are well developed, though there are a few regulatory gaps in Viet Nam in some areas. While the fintech sector has developed several types of lending products that can be useful for WMSMEs, most fintechs do not focus specifically on women and, in fact, many do not track the number of women they serve. Some fintechs focus on WMSMEs because the sector they operate in is dominated by female entrepreneurs. Other than these sector-specific fintechs, there are very few examples of fintechs that intentionally tailor their products for WMSMEs.

There are several reasons why fintechs do not focus on WMSMEs. Some prefer to provide consumer loans, which is perceived to be a more lucrative market. Others believe that the universe of bankable WMSMEs is not large, even though many fintechs do not collect gender data and so are not aware of the characteristics of the WMSME segment.

Fintechs that successfully focus on low-income female entrepreneurs use a combination of online and offline processes, making it easy for WMSMEs to obtain the guidance they require. This results from a focus on building product features especially with female entrepreneurs in mind. More such initiatives are required to reach the large numbers of underserved WMSMEs. Co-lending initiatives that combine the benefits of low-cost bank lending with user-friendly fintech features would be desirable to meet WMSMEs' need for affordability and convenience. Affordability is important because WMSMEs often work in low-margin industries, while convenience is crucial as the entrepreneurs are often constrained for time because of their disproportionate share in care responsibilities.

Besides building specific products and services for WMSMEs, the barriers of low digital and financial literacy and lack of awareness about fintech products also need to be addressed to successfully serve more WMSMEs. This requires coordinated efforts from a range of stakeholders, including industry associations, central banks, fintechs, and banks with cross-sector partnerships and collaborations.

1 INTRODUCTION

Micro, small, and medium-sized enterprises (MSMEs) in developing countries continue to remain underserved despite their significant contribution to their countries' gross domestic product (GDP) and employment. This constrains the MSMEs' growth and negatively impacts their countries' output, employment generation, and income inequality. Within the MSME sector, women-owned MSMEs (WMSMEs)[1] represent the most underserved group. Addressing this gap is imperative to boost each country's GDP and promote positive societal outcomes, including women's empowerment, increased women's employment (Clawson 2023), and enhanced female labor participation rates.

Fintech definition. Financial innovation that makes available new delivery channels, products, and providers is key to expanding access to financial services and reaching underserved populations. In recent times, technology-focused start-ups have been increasingly launching innovative financial products and services historically provided by the traditional financial services industry. As a result, the boundaries of the financial system are getting increasingly blurred, with nonbanks such as telecom companies and technology companies entering the financial services space. Such financial innovations driven by digital technology are often referred to as "fintech."

The Financial Stability Board defines fintech as technologically enabled financial innovation that could result in new business models, applications, processes, or products with an associated material effect on financial markets and institutions, and the provision of financial services.[2] Examples include start-ups that use digital technology to challenge incumbent financial service providers as well as big technology companies that use their data and network advantages gained in nonfinancial service provision to enter the finance sector.

The coronavirus disease (COVID-19) pandemic led to a rapid increase in digitalization and advances in financial technology and resulted in regulations supporting digital finance. These developments represent both an opportunity and a challenge from the financial inclusion perspective. While the challenges of inadequate digital infrastructure and unequal digital access (digital divide) in developing countries need to be addressed, the new paradigm has the potential to provide greater financial access to underserved segments of the population.

Fintech revenue. The fintech sector accounts for only 2% of the global financial services revenue, about $245 billion out of $12.5 trillion, but it is estimated that it will reach $1.5 trillion in annual revenue by 2030 (Boston Consulting Group, 2023). Revenues of banking fintechs (i.e., fintechs that are involved in lending, deposits, payments, and trading and investment services) are projected to grow from 4% to 13% penetration (at a 22% compound annual growth rate) of banking revenue pools by 2030. With 42% of all incremental revenues, the largest market is projected to be the Asia and Pacific region, especially emerging Asia (India, the People's Republic of China, and Southeast Asia), where fintechs are expected to help expand financial inclusion (Boston Consulting Group, 2023).

The purpose of this report is to examine the ways in which fintech is improving access to finance for WMSMEs in Indonesia, the Philippines, and Viet Nam. In addition, the paper discusses the steps that stakeholders can take to make fintech innovations more helpful. The research methodology includes desk research and in-depth interviews with 8–10 sector participants and/or experts in each of the three countries.

---

[1] WMSMEs are defined as firms with more than 50% women's ownership.
[2] Financial Stability Board. FinTech. https://www.fsb.org/work-of-the-fsb/financial-innovation-and-structural-change/fintech/.

2 ISSUES AFFECTING MICRO, SMALL, AND MEDIUM-SIZED ENTERPRISES' ACCESS TO FINANCE

Several factors contribute to the financing challenges for MSMEs in developing countries. MSMEs often lack collateral, financial records, and credit histories—the bases on which lenders make credit assessments.[3] The majority of MSME owners have limited assets and are unable to provide the collateral required by banks as security to obtain loans (International Finance Corporation [IFC] 2012). A second major hurdle is the information opacity prevalent in the MSME sector. Enterprises in the sector are often informal in nature and do not have financial statements. Moreover, as many of them conduct a substantial portion of their business in cash, there are often no records available. This makes preparation of financial statements difficult. A third challenge is that most MSMEs are yet to access formal loans and so do not have credit histories. In their absence, lenders are unable to progress with their credit appraisals. The problem is referred to as "information asymmetry" and contributes to the relatively higher transaction costs for lenders when they deal with this segment. The higher transaction costs arise because the costs of screening MSME borrowers are higher than in the case of larger borrowers, especially when expressed as a percentage of the loan amounts, which typically tend to be relatively smaller. In other words, a very detailed loan appraisal of an MSME based on several site visits and observations may be possible, but this would entail very high transaction costs. Given the smaller unit value of typical MSME loans, such a high transaction cost could make lending to MSMEs unviable. All of these factors make it difficult for MSMEs to access adequate financing.

Even when MSMEs access loans, the amount and tenor of the loans may not suit their needs. MSMEs often need money for working capital but rather than being sanctioned credit lines, they may get term loans based on the amount of collateral they are able to provide. The documentation requirements and lengthy procedures of formal lenders may also be burdensome for MSME owners. Various factors contribute to interest rates on MSME loans being frequently higher than for loans taken out by large corporates (Organisation for Economic Co-operation and Development [OECD] 2022a). The aforementioned higher customer acquisition costs for banks are a contributor. Moreover, the ratings obtained by MSMEs are lower when lending models applied to large enterprises are applied to them, resulting in higher interest rates being charged for loans taken out by them. For instance, MSMEs often lack bargaining power with suppliers and customers, resulting in their having unfavorable working capital terms that are a strain on their liquidity. The high interest rates on the loans they take out further increase the strain on their finances, which contributes to bankers perceiving the MSME sector as risky, resulting in the sector's low share in bank lending. As a result, MSMEs tend to rely on informal lenders who can provide unsecured lending for shorter durations with quick disbursement times, but often at usurious rates of interest.

---

[3] Lenders refer to such borrowers as "thin-file" borrowers.

In Indonesia, financial inclusion is a major challenge with only 52% of adults having a bank account, resulting in 100 million unbanked adults (World Bank 2021). The country has 64.2 million MSMEs[4] contributing 61% to the country's GDP and providing employment to 97% of the total workforce (about 117 million workers) (Rizki 2022). Yet, even in 2020, they received only 20.4% of the total business loans by value, with their share ranging from 21.9% to 19.1% over the last 10 years (OECD 2022b).

In the Philippines, only 51% of adults have financial accounts (World Bank 2021). Hence, financial inclusion is an important goal. There are about 1 million MSMEs in the Philippines,[5] which account for 99.58% of all businesses in the country and 64.7% of the total employment. Microenterprises have the biggest share (32.46%), closely followed by small enterprises (25.08%), while medium-sized enterprises are far behind at 7.12%. The MSME sector contributed 35.7% to the total value added in the country (Philippine Statistics Authority 2022) and about 40% to the GDP (United Nations Development Programme 2020). Yet MSME loans accounted for only 4.9% of total business loans by value in September 2022, well below the 10% mandated by law (Agcaoili 2023). In addition, 67% of MSMEs were reported to be facing credit constraints (BusinessWorld 2023).

In Viet Nam, as per the World Bank's Global Findex Database, 56% of adults had a bank account in 2022. The development of digital financial services enabled expansion in access to financial services in rural areas with limited banking infrastructure, where about 70% of the population lives (Government of Viet Nam Ministry of Finance 2021).

As in the other two countries, MSMEs are an important part of the economy in Viet Nam,[6] accounting for 70% of GDP and 80% of total employment (McKinsey 2022). The financing needs of this segment are again not being adequately addressed by the banks. A 2022 McKinsey report estimates that MSMEs represent a "white space" market constrained by supply, with the opportunity to create an additional D500 trillion ($21 billion) in loan balances for 1 million to 2 million new loan recipients. As of the end of 2022, the credit outstanding to small and medium-sized enterprises (SMEs) accounted for about 19% of the total credit outstanding of the whole economy (State Bank of Vietnam 2023).

In all three countries, MSMEs play an important role in contributing to GDP as well as to employment. Yet, in all three cases, they face challenges of accessing adequate finance. Figure 1 shows the estimated share of MSMEs in total employment in the three countries and Figure 2 shows the share of the MSME sector in GDP and business loans.

---

[4] Small and medium-sized enterprises (SMEs) and MSMEs are defined in Indonesia as enterprises with a maximum turnover of Rp50 billion or maximum assets (excluding building and land assets) of Rp10 billion.

[5] The Philippines employs two criteria in operationally defining MSMEs: (i) employment, and (ii) asset size. The Philippine Statistics Authority classifies an enterprise as a microenterprise if it has fewer than 10 employees, a small enterprise if it has 10–99 employees, a medium-sized enterprise if it has 100–199 employees, and a large enterprise if it has 200 or more employees. On the other hand, Republic Act No. 9501 of 2007 (otherwise known as "the Magna Carta for small enterprises") classifies an enterprise as micro if it has up to ₱3,000,000 in assets, small if it has ₱3,000,001–₱15,000,000 in assets, medium if it has ₱15,000,0001–₱100,000,000 in assets, and large if it has ₱100,000,001 and above in assets size (www.pcw.gov.ph).

[6] Viet Nam's legal definition of an SME includes two criteria: (i) number of employees, and (ii) total revenues or total capital of the business enterprise. For the agriculture, forestry and fishing, and industry and construction sectors, microenterprises have revenue or capital of less than D3 billion and fewer than 10 employees. Small enterprises have up to 100 employees and revenue up to D50 billion or capital up to D20 billion. Medium-sized enterprises have up to 200 employees and revenue up to D300 billion and capital up to D100 billion. For trade and services, microenterprises have fewer than 10 employees, revenue up to D10 billion, and capital up to D3 billion; small enterprises have up to 50 employees, revenue up to D100 billion, and capital up to D50 billion; and medium-sized enterprises have up to 100 employees, revenue up to D300 billion, and capital up to D100 billion (https://www.oecd-ilibrary.org/).

Figure 1: Estimated Share of MSMEs in Total Employment

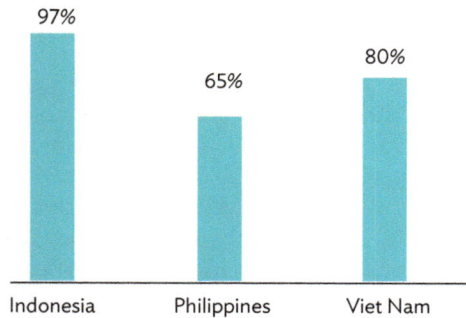

Indonesia: 97%
Philippines: 65%
Viet Nam: 80%

MSME = micro, small, and medium-sized enterprise.

Notes: Based on figures quoted in section 1. Share of business loans is measured as follows:
(i)   Indonesia: Share of total business loans by value.
(ii) Philippines: Share of total business loans by value.
(iii) Viet Nam: Share of the total credit outstanding of the whole economy.

Sources: Rizki 2022; Government of the Philippines Department of Trade and Industry 2022; and McKinsey 2022.

Figure 2: MSME Sector's Share of Gross Domestic Product and Share of Business Loans

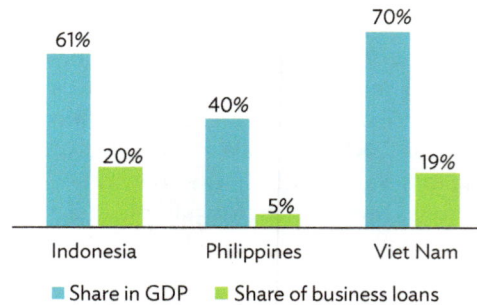

Indonesia: Share in GDP 61%, Share of business loans 20%
Philippines: Share in GDP 40%, Share of business loans 5%
Viet Nam: Share in GDP 70%, Share of business loans 19%

■ Share in GDP   ■ Share of business loans

GDP = gross domestic product; MSME = micro, small, and medium-sized enterprise.

Notes: Based on figures quoted in section 1. Share of business loans is measured as follows:
(i)   Indonesia: Share of total business loans by value.
(ii) Philippines: Share of total business loans by value.
(iii) Viet Nam: Share of the total credit outstanding of the whole economy.

Sources: Rizki 2022; Government of the Philippines Department of Trade and Industry 2022; and McKinsey 2022.

3 CHARACTERISTICS OF WOMEN-OWNED MICRO, SMALL, AND MEDIUM-SIZED ENTERPRISES

According to Statistics Indonesia, an estimated 64.5% of all MSMEs in Indonesia were managed by women as of 2021 (Priyono, Pancawati, and Ginting 2023). Women more often owned micro and small enterprises rather than medium-sized enterprises. WMSMEs in Indonesia tend to operate in the services and trade sectors rather than the manufacturing sector, except for food production (Canada–Indonesia Trade and Private Sector Assistance Project 2019). WMSMEs have also increasingly adopted online selling channels with e-commerce in Southeast Asia tripling in size during 2015–2020, growing to a value of $105 billion (IFC 2021). For example, in Indonesia, one-third of the businesses on the e-commerce platform Lazada were owned by women (IFC 2021). Abdul Latif Jameel Poverty Action Lab analysis suggests that WMSMEs in Indonesia more often use social media rather than formal e-commerce to sell their products, referencing a study that found that 58% of female owners of MSMEs use social media to sell their products or services, while only 17% participate in formal e-commerce marketplaces (Abdul Latif Jameel Poverty Action Lab 2021).

Of the 1 million MSMEs in the Philippines, 30% are reported to be owned by women (IFC 2022a), with this share going up to 45% when only microenterprises are considered. A recent study found that most of the WMSMEs were active in the wholesale and retail trade, accommodation and food services, and manufacturing sectors (Government of the Philippines, Philippine Institute for Development Studies 2023). In the Philippines, too, WMSMEs have increasingly adopted online selling channels. Two-thirds of the businesses on the e-commerce platform Lazada Philippines were owned by women (IFC 2021).

In Viet Nam, about 18% of MSMEs as per Viet Nam General Statistics Office as of December 2020 (Bialus et al. 2022). Women-owned enterprises accounted for 21% of microenterprises, 10% of small enterprises, and 6% of medium-sized enterprises. A study by Hoang and Nguyen (2022) found that nearly 30% of SMEs in Viet Nam were engaged in online selling using social media, specialized apps, or digital platforms. The adoption rates are very similar between women-owned and men-owned SMEs.

In all three countries, WMSMEs are a significant part of the MSME sector with greater representation in the microenterprise category and much lower representation in the other categories. While detailed breakdowns of WMSMEs by sector are not available, in all three countries, retail trade appears to have the highest concentration of WMSMEs. Food services seems to be another popular sector. **Figures 3**, **4**, and **5** show the relative share of female and male ownership of MSMEs in the three countries.

Figure 3: Indonesia: Share in Ownership of MSMEs

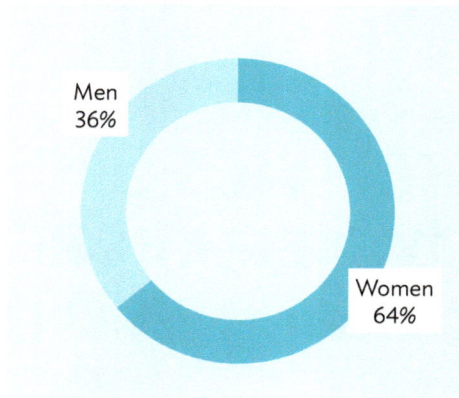

Men 36%

Women 64%

MSMEs = micro, small, and medium-sized enterprises.
Source: Statistics Indonesia 2021.

Figure 4: Philippines: Share in Ownership of MSMEs

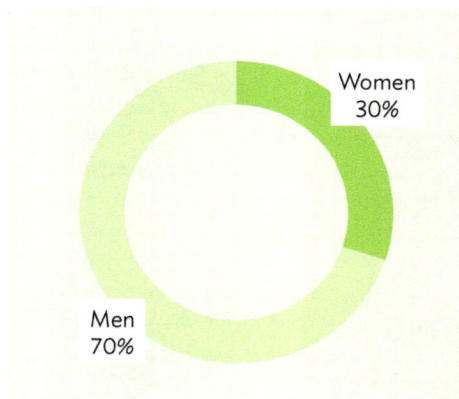

Women 30%

Men 70%

MSMEs = micro, small, and medium-sized enterprises.
Source: IFC 2022.

Figure 5: Viet Nam: Share in Ownership of MSMEs

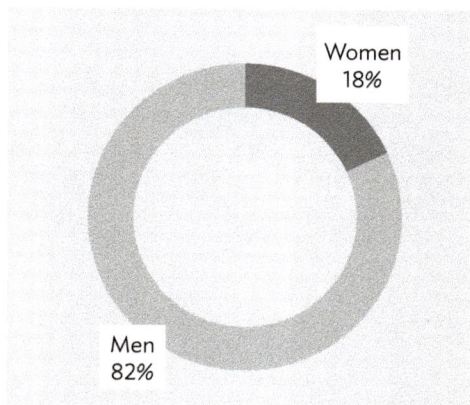

Women 18%

Men 82%

MSMEs = micro, small, and medium-sized enterprises.
Source: Viet Nam General Statistics Office 2021.

4 CHALLENGES OF EXPANDING ACCESS TO FINANCE AND THE POTENTIAL FINTECH SOLUTIONS

While most MSMEs face challenges of accessing finance, WMSMEs face even greater challenges because of the sociocultural and institutional barriers in accessing and using financial services. Most of the barriers are a result of sociocultural practices and societies' perceptions of women, but some barriers are institutional or infrastructure related. Infrastructure-related barriers include women's lack of an identification card to prove their identity, insufficient or absence of traditionally required collateral, mobility constraints, and limited financial literacy. Many of these factors are interrelated and feed into each other. Some sociocultural practices result in women's inability to meet institutional requirements. For instance, women are constrained in their ability to offer collateral because most often family property is in the name of male members of the family. Women's lack of financial literacy results in their inability to complete bank documentation. For instance, in Viet Nam, bank officers report that poor loan documentation, particularly inaccurate and incomplete data on the company's financial health, is one of the main reasons for rejecting women entrepreneurs' loan applications (Bialus et al. 2022).

Other barriers to women's account ownership include their concerns about account maintenance costs, perceptions of account utility, lack of sex-disaggregated data on financial product usage that prevents institutions from learning about the specific banking needs of women, insufficient financial products tailored to women's needs, lack of credit history, and the high costs of dealing with financial service providers (Asian Development Bank [ADB] 2022).

The World Bank's Women, Business and the Law Project scores countries on an index that assesses the gender equality of laws and regulations. An indicator relating to assets examines gender differences in property and inheritance law. A score of 100 indicates that women are on an equal legal standing with men. Viet Nam scored a 100 but Indonesia scored 60 and the Philippines 75, indicating that there are gaps, especially in Indonesia (World Bank n.d.).

Because of all these factors, the WMSME market is severely underserved, and, as a result, it represents a large opportunity for financial service providers. Financial institutions that serve women intentionally have found women to be good savers and borrowers and loyal customers (Financial Alliance for Women 2021a). The global finance gap for WMSMEs is estimated to range from $1.4 trillion to $1.7 trillion (IFC 2022b).

In Indonesia, the financing gap for WMSMEs (92% of which are microenterprises) is estimated to be $6 billion (Women Entrepreneurs Finance Initiative 2019). The main barrier is reported to be lack of physical collateral (Centennial Asia Advisors and Independent Research & Advisory Indonesia 2018). In the Philippines, according to the Bangko Sentral ng Pilipinas (BSP), 58% of WMSMEs cited lack of access to funding as an issue in doing business, as against 37% of men-owned MSMEs (BusinessWorld 2023). In Viet Nam, a study found that 41% of the WMSMEs surveyed had not taken a business loan (Bialus et al. 2022). While 65% of those who had not taken a loan were not interested in bank finance, the remaining WMSMEs wanted to access bank financing. However, they faced difficulties because of the complex application and cumbersome requirements, particularly in terms of providing hard collateral.

To adequately serve women, financial service providers must first understand women's financial service needs and then make appropriate adjustments to their products and services. This is sometimes referred to as making financial services more "gender intelligent" or "gender smart."

In the context of financing WMSMEs, studies have indicated that the following features of loan products are especially important to reach female customers:

(i) **Flexibility** with collateral requirements, such as acceptance of moveable collateral instead of fixed assets, may help some women access loans. Loans that rely on other criteria such as transaction histories or digital data trails have the potential to serve more women.

(ii) **Accessibility** is important to address the challenges women face because of their multiple roles and extensive unpaid care duties as highlighted by an International Labour Organization study that revealed 4.1-fold disparity in care work between women and men in Asia and the Pacific (International Labour Organization 2018). Given women's mobility constraints, the geographic distance to the closest bank branch or ATM further limits women running micro and very small enterprises (AFI 2023), thereby hindering their financial inclusion.

(iii) **Affordability** of financing is critical, as WMSMEs tend to predominantly work in low-margin businesses such as retail trade. High interest rates and fees make loans unviable (Bialus et al. 2022).

(iv) **Provision** of greater guidance on products and services would help women MSME owners, who tend to be more cautious and prudent, in making borrowing decisions (Bialus et al. 2022) The finding in World Bank's Global Findex 2021 report that unbanked women lack the confidence to navigate financial services without help may apply to underserved female MSME owners too.

(v) **Simple documentation requirements** would enable women, especially those lacking financial literacy and time (AFI 2023), to apply for loans. Having easier documentation could also reduce the prospect of their applications being rejected because of administrative reasons.

(vi) **Integrating nonfinancial services** to complement financial institutions' core financial offerings for WMSMEs can help mitigate some of the barriers they face in accessing loans. Examples of nonfinancial services are providing business-related information, business and financial education, and advice and mentoring. Facilitating access to networking tools and events and providing business management technology (such as for invoicing or payroll) are other important examples. An analysis of five SME banking models indicated that well-integrated nonfinancial services for women-owned SMEs yielded positive return on investment within 1 to 2 years (IFC–Netherlands Development Finance Company 2020).

Fintech solutions have scope to provide these features. For instance, fintechs often draw on transaction histories and data trails that could reduce the need for hard collateral. As their services are online, there are typically no barriers on account of geographic distance. They also have scope to offer more affordable financing as they may be able to save on costs because of their lower need for physical infrastructure. Finally, fintechs can use technology to develop innovative ways to address WMSME owners' need for guidance, reduce the burden of loan documentation requirements, and provide nonfinancial services economically.

The fintech sector is fairly developed in all three countries with the pandemic having given a boost to MSME digitalization and participation in e-commerce platforms, though there are gaps in Viet Nam's regulatory framework causing it to lag in some areas. Indonesia was ranked 43rd in findexable's Global Fintech rankings and had about 850 fintech firms as per the Robocash Group's SEA-2022: State of Fintech report. The Philippines was ranked 53rd in findexable's Global Fintech rankings and had about 230 fintech firms, while Viet Nam was ranked 70th in findexable's Global Fintech rankings and had about 207 fintech firms.

All three countries have high electricity coverage, internet penetration, social media usage, cell phone usage (including considerable smartphone usage), suggesting that fintech solutions have substantial scope to reach a wide segment of the population. (**Appendix 1** provides recent statistics for the countries on the above parameters). Women in low- and middle-income countries are 7% less likely than men to own a mobile phone, 17% are less likely than men to own a smartphone, and 19% are less likely than men to use mobile internet (GSM Association 2023). The main barriers are affordability, lack of digital literacy, lack of perceived relevance, and internet safety concerns. Yet the availability of fintech infrastructure and the large number of women using mobile phones and the internet in these countries indicate considerable potential to leverage fintech solutions to improve financial access for women.

In Indonesia, Bank Indonesia, the central bank, and the Financial Services Authority (OJK) oversee the fintech sector. In the Philippines, the central bank, BSP, and the Philippines Securities and Exchange Commission regulate the sector while in Viet Nam, the regulator is the central bank, the State Bank of Vietnam.

Regulators in all three countries are broadly supportive of the fintech sector because of the benefits that it can provide for the economy, though Viet Nam is yet to issue certain regulations that could help the sector grow. In Indonesia and the Philippines, fintechs can participate in regulatory sandboxes to test new financial innovations.[7] In Viet Nam, a draft decree for a regulatory sandbox was introduced in 2022 but is yet to be implemented. The country also does not yet have regulations governing peer-to-peer (P2P) lending (Acclime Vietnam 2023).

While mobile phone ownership among women is high in all three countries, in Indonesia, there is an 11% difference in the proportions of the male and female populations that own a mobile phone. (Economic Research Institute for ASEAN and East Asia 2021). Moreover, even though digital penetration may be high, consumers may be using their smartphones primarily to access social media apps such as Facebook, TikTok, or WhatsApp, or consumer tech apps such as Gojek, Grab, or Lazada. They may still lack digital security skills such as protecting passwords, identifying misinformation, and spotting fraud, which may lead to a higher number of customers falling prey to scams and predatory lenders. This in turn can have the effect of limiting confidence in digital financial services as being untrustworthy or not secure (Centre for Impact Investing and Practices [CIIP] 2023). A 2021 study based on data from 28 countries found that 29% of men use fintech products and services compared with 21% of women, which shows a gender gap in almost every country (Chen et al. 2021).

---

[7] A regulatory sandbox refers to a controlled, time-bound live testing environment, which may feature regulatory waivers.

5 FINTECH-ENABLED BUSINESS MODELS

A range of fintech-enabled business models has emerged, several of which are already offering loans or have scope to offer loans to WMSMEs.[8] The models differ based on various parameters, but three important differentiating factors are (i) the regulatory structures of the financial service provider, (ii) the method of loan origination and extent of digitalization used in the business model, and (iii) the source of funding. The models are summarized in **Table 1** and described in the sections below.

Table 1: Fintech-Enabled Business Models That Can Expand Women-Owned Micro, Small, and Medium-Sized Enterprises' Financial Access

Basis for Differentiating Fintech Models	Types of Fintech Models Based on the Differentiating Factor
Regulatory structure of financial service provider	(i) Peer-to-peer lending platforms
	(ii) Digital wallets
	(iii) Digital banks
	(iv) Nonfinancial fintech companies offering financing
Method of loan origination and degree of digitalization involved	Entirely digital
	Hybrid or "phygital"
Source of funding	Lending by fintech start-ups
	Lending by fintech subsidiaries of banks
	Fintech-bank co-lending
	Peer-to-peer lending

fintech = financial technology.
Source: Authors.

A. Regulatory Structure of Financial Service Provider

Based on the regulatory permissions that fintechs have, the four main categories of fintech players include P2P lending platforms, digital wallets, digital banks, and nonfinancial companies.

1. Peer-to-Peer Lending Platforms

P2P lending platforms match funders with individuals or small firms looking for external funding and are sometimes referred to as marketplace lending or platform lending. Typically, applicants registering on the platform go through a standardized screening process. Funders can choose which applicant to fund and how much to fund them for. The platforms work mainly as a conduit and generally do not have direct credit risk exposure to the loans. They principally generate revenue from loan origination and servicing fees (Beck 2020).

---

[8] **Appendix 2** lists the fintechs mentioned in this publication and provides details of their year of launch, primary service, and legal and/or regulatory status.

Individuals and, at times, institutional investors can fund individuals or small firms whose profiles are on the platforms. Although known as the P2P model, some players, such as Amartha in Indonesia, have also incorporated an institutional-to-peer model on their platform. As demand for loans continues to increase, P2P lending is unable to fulfill the needs of the borrowers, especially considering the seasonal behavior of individual lenders resulting in uncertain capital supply. Engaging with institutional lenders to support the growing demand for loans provides a more stable source of funding with capabilities to provide higher ticket sizes. Thus, by having institutional lenders, players can serve more borrowers and expand their MSME coverage.

P2P lending offers an avenue for WMSMEs to obtain financing, as loans are typically collateral free. Most P2P platforms serve both men and women, though a few, such as Amartha, focus only on women. Modalku is an Indonesian P2P lending platform that focuses on MSMEs. In Indonesia, there are more than 30 million active P2P borrower accounts (Boston Consulting Group 2023). Within this space, the regulator, OJK, has recognized a category of Sharia-based P2P lenders catering to those seeking Islamic finance options. An example from the Philippines is Blend.ph, which provides an online marketplace connecting those seeking funds with financial institutions and investors. In Viet Nam, Validus is an online unsecured lending platform that focuses specifically on SMEs.

2. Digital Wallets

Digital wallets (also known as electronic wallets or e-wallets) allow users to store digital money and use it to make transactions online and at merchants and businesses that accept e-wallets. Mobile wallets are a type of digital wallet especially designed for use on mobile devices.

Digital wallet services can use their network and digital trails to enable access to finance for underserved segments. For example, in the Philippines the mobile wallet space is dominated by GCash, the country's biggest mobile wallet with 76 million registered users (67% of the population). GCash provides its users with accessible credit lines that can be used for QR code-based and online payments. The loan product (GCredit) is overseen by GCash's credit affiliate, Fuse Lending, which also runs the company's other digital lending products (Fintech News Philippines 2023). More than 50% of GCash users are estimated to be women, including many who are owners of neighborhood shops (known locally as sari-sari stores), and they act as a channel for GCash offering cash-in, cash-out, bills payment, and fund transfer services (Manila Standard 2022). The large outreach of GCash in the Philippines makes it an ideal partner for banks seeking to reach underserved communities. For example, UNO Digital Bank in the Philippines has partnered with GCash to reach potential customers. The partnership allows GCash customers to open an UNO Digital Bank account directly from the GCash app and access UNO Digital Bank products through it.

3. Digital Banks

Digital banks are regulated and licensed banks that offer most services of traditional banks, exclusively online with no physical branches. They have lower operational costs on account of limited physical infrastructure and their ability to scale up rapidly on account of automation. Moreover, digital banks have an opportunity to cross-sell products based on transactional data. The value proposition that these banks offer to customers is access to a broad range of banking services in an efficient manner with nimble customer-facing processes and services. Like traditional banks, digital banks earn revenues from intermediation margins, fees, and charges.

Three main types of digital banks include digitally native challenger banks (also sometimes referred to as neobanks), digitized incumbent banks, and greenfield banks launched as an offshoot of an incumbent bank (Jenik and Zetterli 2020). All three countries have several neo banks—Bank Neo Commerce in Indonesia, Tonik Bank in the Philippines, and Timo Digital Bank in Viet Nam. A good example of a digitized incumbent bank is Bank Jago in Indonesia, formerly known as Bank Artos Indonesia. The bank became a digitized bank on acquiring investment from the ride-hailing tech start-up Gojek, enabling it to directly offer digital banking services through the Gojek app. On the other hand, UnionDigital Bank in the Philippines and digibank in Indonesia are examples of greenfield digital banks launched as offshoots of incumbent banks; UnionDigital Bank was launched by UnionBank and digibank by DBS Bank, Singapore.

Many digital banks leverage alternate credit scores and/or proprietary algorithms to extend online loans to individuals and entrepreneurs. For example, UNO Digital Bank in the Philippines has a partnership with artificial intelligence fintech Trusting Social, which provides consumer credit insights based on telco data in order to assess potential customers, many of whom may be unbanked. Because of their use of alternate data, digital banks could be a source of financing for underserved segments such as WMSMEs. However, a 2020 study found that even in a developed country like the United Kingdom, men are more likely to have a digital bank account compared to women, with a difference of 3 percentage points (AltFi 2020).

4. Nonfinancial Fintech Companies Offering Financing

Fintech innovations have enabled nonfinancial companies to offer financial products and services that are sometimes referred to as "embedded finance." In the lending space, the most common example of this development is the provision of short-term credit for purchase of inventory. Fintech companies, such as digital wallet providers, e-commerce, or business-to-business platforms, have high-frequency and exclusive data on merchants and consumers, many of whom are underserved by banks. This has motivated many of them to offer merchants or small businesses short-term credit in the form of business inventory loans allowing merchants to defer payments into one or more installments. For example, Growsari, a technology-enabled business-to-business platform, serves about 23,000 MSME corner stores (known locally as sari-sari stores) and enables them to procure inventory and access financial services. It offers a financial product that enables its customers to buy higher-value products on credit. Stocking these higher-value items, typically tobacco and liquor items, has the potential to increase the store's revenues.

Fairbanc, a Singapore-based fintech company operating in Indonesia, is in a similar sector. Its customers are typically last-mile micro-merchants who purchase $50–$300 of several large brands' products per week. As these entities are unable to access credit from formal sources, inventory is typically purchased through cash at hand or by borrowing from informal lenders, which is a major barrier to buying more goods. Through its business inventory "buy now, pay later" (BNPL) loans solution, Fairbanc removes this constraint and allows the mom-and-pop stores to buy more stock, which they can pay for after they have sold to their customers. The increase in inventory leads to growth in sales, which then starts a positive reinforcing loop through an increased credit line and more purchases. In addition, Fairbanc provides closed-loop financing, which requires no cash exchange. Instead, the credit provided is used only to purchase inventory, ensuring that the financing the borrowers receive is always productive and reinvested into their business. Fairbanc has partnerships with several fast-moving consumer goods (FMCGs) companies such as Unilever to reach and connect with the small merchants that sell their merchandise. These FMCG companies allow access to their merchants because integrating Fairbanc's BNPL solution increases inventory purchases of merchants, which in turn leads to top-line growth (Limcaoco 2021). Fairbanc analyzes historical data on each merchant from FMCG companies to offer a dynamic credit line that is regularly updated based on the merchant's performance. According to a survey done by Unilever and Fairbanc, 80% of Fairbanc's end users are unbanked and about 70% are women (Shu 2022).

A study by Bian, Cong, and Ji (2023) on e-wallets in the People's Republic of China found that e-wallet credit or BNPL loans have expanded financial access for underserved communities, especially for women and those in rural areas. As the eligibility criteria for these loans are typically not difficult to meet, they can provide a credit option for financially excluded individuals. Though data on the gender distribution of such loans is not available, the higher approval rates for BNPL loans compared to other kinds of loans may make it more accessible for women entrepreneurs who need short-term financing (Shou-Zibell and Corley 2022). The concern with BNPL loans is that soft credit checks may result in overborrowing and repayment stress, especially in countries with several BNPL providers, as these loans are not reported to credit bureaus.

All the above models are observed in the three countries, and a trend of banks increasingly being interested in partnering with fintech companies is also observed.

B. Method of Loan Origination and Degree of Digitalization Involved

Another way to differentiate between fintech models is by examining the method of loan origination and degree of digitalization involved. In some cases, the entire financing process from end-to-end is digital, while in other cases there is a blending of digital experiences with physical interactions at one or more stages of the process. These blended hybrid models are sometimes referred to as "phygital" models. A good example of a "phygital" model is GoTyme Bank in the Philippines, which is a digital bank but offers a combination of physical and digital systems. Kiosks staffed by bank ambassadors are in retail locations of a national supermarket chain and offer customers instant account opening services and a free debit card (GoTyme Bank 2023).

The major advantage of greater digitalization is that it allows transactions across a larger geographical area and reduces the requirement for the financial service provider to have physical infrastructure and field force in various locations, thus decreasing their costs. It also allows transactions without having to rely on personal relationships, which helps increase transparency. However, blending in some physical interactions through the process may have benefits in making the process easier and more user friendly. In the context of financing of WMSMEs, more digital features can help break down geographic barriers to financial inclusion and could enable reduction of financial service providers' lending costs and improve affordability of loans for WMSMEs. Including some degree of physical interaction may, however, help in providing convenience to women entrepreneurs, enable them to receive the guidance they need, and enhance their confidence in accessing the financial product.

Some of the companies that successfully serve WMSMEs in rural areas use a combination of online and offline processes. For example, in Indonesia, Amartha, a licensed P2P lending platform with roots in conventional microfinance, focuses on rural, low-income female borrowers using a hybrid model. The company's field officers help implement a group lending model like that used by Grameen Bank. The officers help verify and validate details of potential applicants or borrowers for the P2P platform. They quantify each physical asset that borrowers have and then, using the company's proprietary algorithm, they develop credit scores for them. The credit scores depend on the type of business and its size and location. The agents also help physically complete know-your-customer requirements. Profiles of MSMEs that achieve a certain minimum credit score are uploaded on the P2P platform through which they can access loans from individuals as well as institutions. The company calls this model an "offline-to-online" model.

Similarly, in the Philippines, Growsari (mentioned earlier), whose customers are primarily women (85%), offers offline support for them. Though all Growsari transactions are conducted through the platform, the company supports new customers with a training team whose members visit the locations of these new customers. The team members do not take orders themselves but train the customer to place the order through the app. Until August 2021, the sari-sari store owners ordered inventory through the platform but paid cash on delivery to the truckers transporting their orders. Since August 2021, the company has started offering the stores credit for higher-value products and the option to use digital payments. However not all stores use digital payments because of infrastructure gaps, such as stores' inability to access phone signals, data, or Wi-Fi in some areas at times. In addition, their internet connections may not always be good enough to carry out digital transactions (CIIP 2023).

C.   Source of Funding

Another important differentiating factor between fintech models that provide financing is the source of funding for loans. Four common types of models exist.

In the first model, fintech start-ups borrow money from financial institutions to make loans. The fintechs in this model generate revenue from both origination fees and interest income. An example of a financial technology start-up that uses this model is the Indonesian digital lender JULO, which has a digital data-driven credit underwriting and risk assessment platform to process consumer credit applications and determine their creditworthiness using its mobile app.

The second model is of incumbent banks directly providing funding through their fintech initiatives. For example, UnionBank of the Philippines has a wholly owned fintech subsidiary, UBX Philippines Corporation. UBX has an online lending marketplace, SeekCap, in which not only UnionBank but 15 other partner financial institutions and banks participate.

A third model involves fintech companies partnering with incumbent banks to provide financing. In this model, sometimes referred to as a co-lending model, banks collaborate with nonbanks and leverage the nonbanks' fintech tools to extend credit to previously unbanked sections of the economy. The use of alternative credit rating systems and machine learning by fintechs has the potential to reduce banks' lending risks and expand their customer base. For example, in Indonesia, AMAAN, a fintech company that focuses on women microentrepreneurs, partners with Bank Jago, an Indonesian bank providing digital banking services. This enables AMAAN's customers to access financing solutions seamlessly and conveniently (CIIP 2023). In Viet Nam, KiotViet, a fintech company supplying cloud-based store management software, has entered into partnerships with multiple banks with the objective of facilitating financial access for the 200,000 microenterprises and small businesses it serves.

A fourth model is the P2P model in which funding is usually received by borrowers directly from individuals and at times institutional investors. Amartha in Indonesia, Blend.ph in the Philippines, and Validus in Viet Nam are examples of this model. Borrowing from P2P platforms usually requires borrowers to pay significant origination fees ranging from 1% to 8% depending upon the platform in addition to the interest rate on the loan. This could have an impact on the affordability of the loans. However, the benefits of P2P lending are that it is usually collateral free and convenient.

In general, fintech players tend to offer products with shorter tenures and higher annualized prices than traditional banks. Fintech interest rates are higher because their cost of funds is typically more than that of a bank. However, fintech company interfaces and user experiences are usually better than those of incumbent banks, as leveraging technology is straightforward and not constrained by existing legacy systems and cultures. Moreover, the nature of products offered by traditional banks may not suit MSME customers. For example, Modalku, the P2P lender in Indonesia mentioned earlier, found that MSME customers often come to them instead of banks because customers need quick fund disbursement that is also collateral free (CIIP 2023).

In a partnership model between fintechs and banks, customers benefit from lower borrowing costs and convenience, both of which are important factors for WMSMEs.

The four models are pictorially represented in Figure 6.

Figure 6: Partnership Models between Fintechs and Banks

Model 1: Lending by Fintech Start-ups

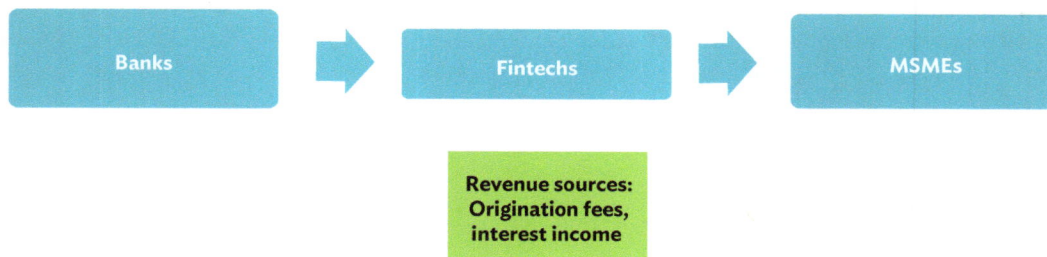

Banks → Fintechs → MSMEs

Revenue sources: Origination fees, interest income

Model 2: Lending by Fintech Subsidiaries of Banks

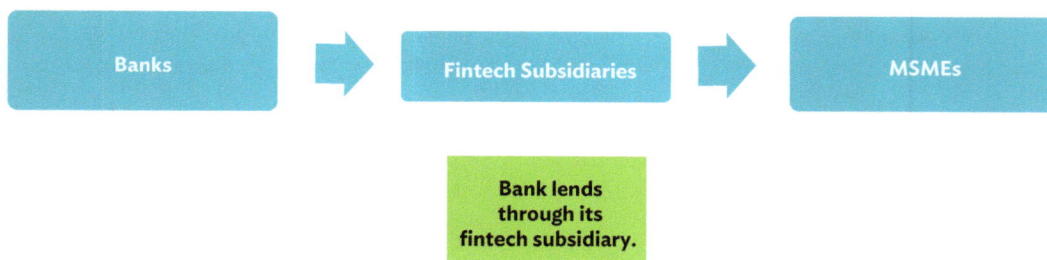

Banks → Fintech Subsidiaries → MSMEs

Bank lends through its fintech subsidiary.

Model 3: Fintech–Bank Co-lending Model

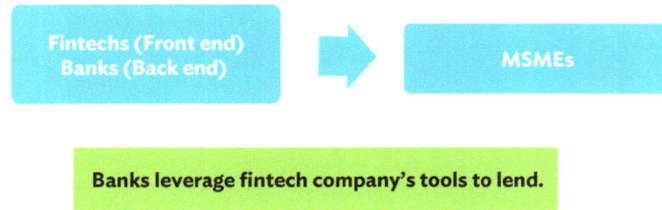

| Fintechs (Front end) Banks (Back end) | → | MSMEs |

Banks leverage fintech company's tools to lend.

Model 4: P2P Lending

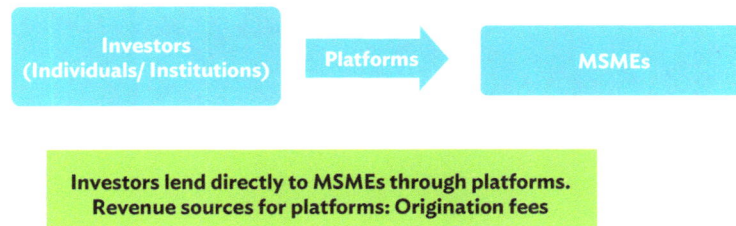

| Investors (Individuals/ Institutions) | Platforms → | MSMEs |

Investors lend directly to MSMEs through platforms.
Revenue sources for platforms: Origination fees

fintechs = financial technology companies; MSMEs = micro, small, and medium-sized enterprises; P2P = peer-to-peer.
Source: Authors.

6 FINTECH LENDING PROCESSES AND ENABLING TECHNOLOGIES

A. Fintech Lending Processes

In an entirely digital loan, digital innovations can be used throughout the lending process. All stages of the loan are completed through digital channels using digitized data and cashless transactions (Figure 7). Using digitized data, digital lenders can formulate decisions on credit applications and enhance customer engagement. Disbursement and collection can be done remotely through digital wallets. Machine learning algorithms and automation can also be incorporated into the digital lending process. However, care needs to be taken to ensure that there is no gender-based algorithmic bias because, in some cases, it has been found that the algorithm creates results that are systemically prejudiced against certain people, with gender explaining the bias. Technology, along with effective management and organizational processes can provide solutions for bias mitigation (Kelly and Mirpourian 2021). There is a case for organizations to invest in building cross-functional teams to actively work with data scientists and develop and articulate mitigation strategies and implement them.

Figure 7: Digital Loan Process

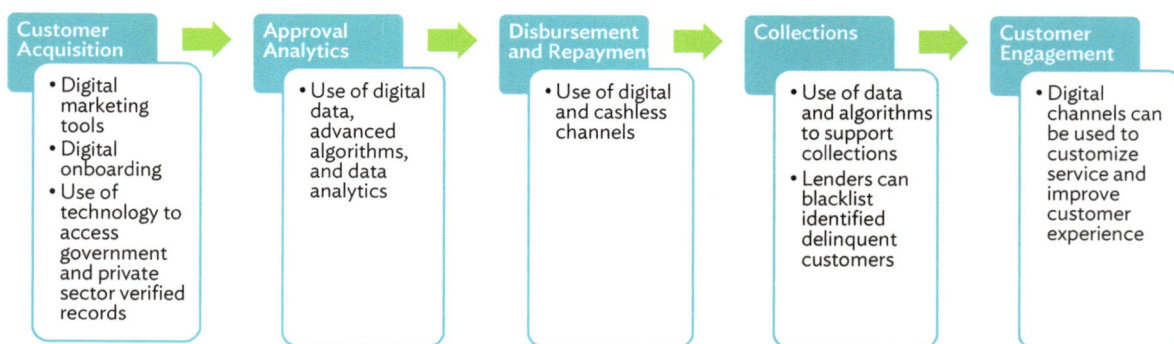

Customer Acquisition	Approval Analytics	Disbursement and Repayment	Collections	Customer Engagement
• Digital marketing tools • Digital onboarding • Use of technology to access government and private sector verified records	• Use of digital data, advanced algorithms, and data analytics	• Use of digital and cashless channels	• Use of data and algorithms to support collections • Lenders can blacklist identified delinquent customers	• Digital channels can be used to customize service and improve customer experience

Source: Quimba, Barral, and Carlos 2023.

A CIIP (2023) study found that the three most digitized or automated practices are (i) know-your-customer compliance and onboarding; (ii) credit risk assessment practices including underwriting, credit scoring, and loan approval; and (iii) direct loan disbursements to borrowers. Past repayment behavior, cash flow analyses, and payroll or employment data were the most used for underwriting, though some fintechs also tap into alternative data such as in-app behaviors, transaction or purchasing data, or telco data in their credit appraisals. For example, the Indonesian

MSME digital financing platform Modalku triangulates alternative data sources, such as e-commerce data, invoicing data, payments data, and mobile data, to assess the creditworthiness of its borrowers. This helps Modalku work around deficiencies in credit bureau data, especially since its underserved customer base is often not covered by these databases (CIIP 2023). Similarly, credit-led MSME neobank KoinWorks in Indonesia uses not only bank and financial statements and credit bureau information, but also looks at a company's digital footprint. By partnering with e-commerce platforms, KoinWorks can examine historical sales data points to assess the creditworthiness of its borrowers. These forms of alternative credit scoring have been able to increase access to capital loans for previously underserved MSME customers.

A separate category of fintech companies has emerged that specializes in providing alternate credit scoring models. These alternate credit scoring models are most often based on anonymized data obtained from telecom operators about mobile usage and bill payments. For example, FinScore, a fintech company in the Philippines analyzes more than 400 telecom data variables (such as data and voice usage, top-up patterns, location, and device data) to predict a customer's creditworthiness. In addition, the company provides a tool for fraud detection and social media lookup. Besides telco data, data relating to tax records, utility bill payments, and data from payment gateways and e-commerce sites may also be used to develop alternate credit scores.

Providers of alternate credit scores typically collaborate with lenders who can use the scores to base their digital lending decisions. Often these scores are sold by the fintech companies to lenders for a fee. Alternate credit scoring is important in the context of WMSMEs who are unable to provide hard collateral. It is hard to determine the exact percentage of women who benefit from telco-based credit scores as telco data usually do not contain gender information. Trusting Social (mentioned earlier), which provides consumer credit insights based on telco behavior, found through an internal 2020 study on its Viet Nam operations that women are a large part of its credit-enabled database. It also found that women had higher approval rates for loans compared to men for digital-first lending, where the borrower's gender was not used as a filter for decision-making and they did not need to go in person to apply for a loan. The study found that the company's alternate credit scores helped good borrowers get continued credit access, with nearly 40% of consumers getting multiple loan offers over 12 months. Trusting Social also helped borrowers migrate from unlicensed moneylenders to formal lending at lower interest rates, since the company only works with regulated lenders.

B. Enabling Technologies

Specific features of fintech applications can help or hinder accessibility for unbanked entrepreneurs.

1. Intuitive and User-Friendly

Applications need to be intuitive and user-friendly to encourage adoption and usage among the target population. In the case of WMSMEs, this is especially important given their need for convenience and ease of operation. The user interface of the application must be in the local and/or regional language and be easy to use for those with low levels of literacy. In some locations this means that the application should not require a smartphone but could also run on feature phones.

2. Lightweight and Offline

To cater to low-income individuals who may have phones with lower memory capacities, the application should not occupy a large part of the phone memory. A good example of such an application is that of BukuWarung, an Indonesian fintech providing bookkeeping, digital payments, and e-commerce solutions for MSMEs in Indonesia. While talking to MSMEs, BukuWarung's founders realized that many were using pay-as-you-go data plans and lower-end smartphones. This led them to focus on making their application as lightweight as possible and enabling it to work offline so users could access and update their records anytime. This focus on making their app take up as little data and space as possible differentiated their app from competing digital ledger apps and helped them sign up and retain users in Indonesia (Shu 2020).

3. Affordable

Affordability of financial services are important criterion for WMSMEs, financial solutions must be delivered in a low-cost manner. Cloud-based services offer an important way for fintechs to reduce costs and improve operational efficiency and scalability (Schou-Zibell and Husar 2023). Cloud computing is a scalable, elastic, and on-demand service providing access to servers, storage, networks, software, and analytics over the internet. This is particularly useful for new digital banks and fintech start-ups still testing their technology and business models, as it provides flexibility to scale capacity up or down to accommodate peak periods. Software as a service providers typically handle maintenance, updates, and security, resulting in lower up-front and operational costs. The security of cloud-based systems depends on the specific provider and the security measures they have in place, so financial service providers need to make a careful evaluation of the provider and their security measures prior to moving critical data to the cloud. In some cases, cloud computing can enhance security in core banking through secure and scalable infrastructure and access to advanced security features, such as encryption and two-factor authentication. Cloud providers may also have built-in disaster recovery and business continuity capabilities, which can help financial service providers avoid costly downtime during an outage. As data is stored in a secure, off-site location, it may not be affected by local disasters.

A good example of the use of cloud computing services is that of Cantilan Bank, a rural bank in the Philippines, which operates entirely from a secure cloud-based infrastructure network. This has enabled it to pass on cost savings to consumers and enhance the customer experience. Cloud computing also enabled the bank to reestablish connections immediately following the devastating impact of Typhoon Rai on Surigao del Sur and the rest of the Caraga region in December 2021 (Schou-Zibell and Husar 2023)

7 FINTECH COMPANIES' CURRENT FOCUS ON WOMEN-OWNED MICRO, SMALL, AND MEDIUM-SIZED ENTERPRISES

While the fintech sector has developed several types of lending products that can be useful for WMSMEs, most fintechs do not focus specifically on women and, in fact, some do not track the number of women they serve. To understand female customers better, fintechs need to start collecting and analyzing sex-disaggregated data (Financial Alliance for Women 2021b). **Figure 8** summarizes the different factors that affect fintech financing for WMSMEs.

Figure 8: Factors Affecting Fintech Women-Owned Micro, Small, and Medium-Sized Enterprise Financing

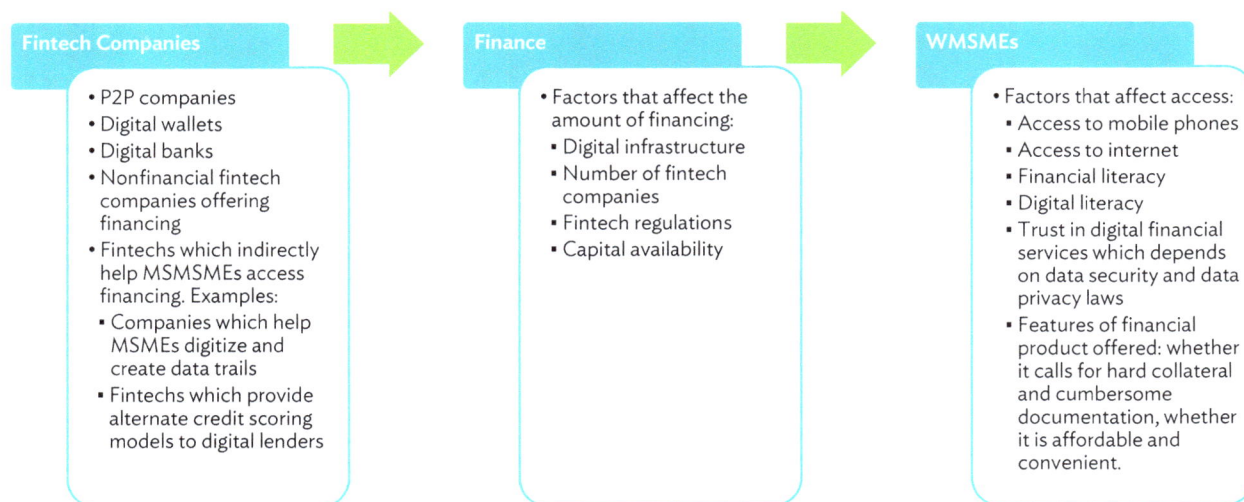

Fintech Companies	Finance	WMSMEs
• P2P companies • Digital wallets • Digital banks • Nonfinancial fintech companies offering financing • Fintechs which indirectly help MSMSMEs access financing. Examples: ▪ Companies which help MSMEs digitize and create data trails ▪ Fintechs which provide alternate credit scoring models to digital lenders	• Factors that affect the amount of financing: ▪ Digital infrastructure ▪ Number of fintech companies ▪ Fintech regulations ▪ Capital availability	• Factors that affect access: ▪ Access to mobile phones ▪ Access to internet ▪ Financial literacy ▪ Digital literacy ▪ Trust in digital financial services which depends on data security and data privacy laws • Features of financial product offered: whether it calls for hard collateral and cumbersome documentation, whether it is affordable and convenient.

MSMEs = micro, small, and medium-sized enterprises; P2P = peer-to-peer.
Source: Authors.

A. Types of Women-Owned Micro, Small, and Medium-Sized Enterprise-Focused Fintechs

1. Fintechs That Intentionally Focus on Women-Owned Micro, Small, and Medium-Sized Enterprises

There are not many examples of fintech companies that intentionally focus on financing WMSMEs. Indonesian P2P lender Amartha (mentioned earlier) is a rare example of a fintech company that specifically focuses on WMSMEs. The company provides women entrepreneurs loans ranging in size from $250 to $1,000 with a 1-year tenor, solely for productive purposes. Another young Indonesian fintech company, Amaan (mentioned earlier), also focuses on women microentrepreneurs.[9] Yet another Indonesian fintech company that solely focuses on women, though not necessarily women entrepreneurs, is Mapan, a digital rotating savings and credit organization (locally called arisan in Indonesia).[10] Mapan's members save regularly and can make a big-ticket purchase when it is their turn to receive funds. Using the company's app, the member can choose from a catalog of items. Mapan has a tie-up with suppliers and has the item delivered to the member the next day. While most of the items in the catalog are household products, there are some items such as cold freezers and pasta makers that are purchased by microentrepreneurs for their businesses. Mapan, however, does not provide loans but only enables women to save and make big-ticket purchases.

2. Fintechs That Focus on Women-Owned Micro, Small, and Medium-Sized Enterprises Because They Operate in Women-Owned Micro, Small, and Medium-Sized Enterprise-Dominated Sectors

Some fintechs focus on women entrepreneurs because the sector in which they operate is dominated by WMSMEs. As Filipino corner stores are often run by women, they account for about 85% of the customers of Growsari (mentioned earlier). Similarly, 70% of the customers of Fairbanc (mentioned earlier), whose customers are micro-merchants in Indonesia, are women because many of the corner stores are run by women.

B. Reasons Why Many Fintechs Do Not Focus on Women-Owned Micro, Small, and Medium-Sized Enterprises

Other than fintechs that operate in WMSME-dominated sectors, there are very few examples of fintechs that focus especially on financing WMSMEs and providing them tailor-made services. The reasons for this are as follows:

1. Greater Interest in Consumer Lending

Many fintech lenders focus on consumer lending (which is basically lending to individuals to finance household, family, and other personal expenditures) rather than on business lending. This is because the market for consumer lending is perceived to be larger than the bankable MSME segment and is also considered easier to service. However, some of these loans may still be channeled to MSMEs as often loans are taken out by the individual entrepreneur but used for the business. For example, loans from the Indonesian digital lender JULO (mentioned earlier) may be used for any purpose, but 40% of its loans are estimated to be used for business purposes.

---

[9] The company was founded in 2021.

[10] In a rotating savings and credit association, a group of individuals makes set contributions to a common fund on a regular basis (usually monthly) for a period. Every month, one member withdraws the fund.

2. Perception That the Universe of Bankable Women-Owned Micro, Small, and Medium-Sized Enterprises Is Not Large

Most digital lending companies do not particularly focus on women because the universe of bankable WMSMEs is not perceived to be large. As a result, many do not consider it worthwhile to collect data on the gender distribution of the customers they serve. An example of a fintech company focused on MSMEs is First Circle in the Philippines, which offers collateral-free credit lines for working capital to MSMEs that have been operating for at least 6 months and have revenue of at least ₱5 million ($92,000). The company does not collect data on the gender distribution of the entrepreneurs it serves. However, some fintechs that do collect gender data find that female entrepreneurs make up a substantial percentage of their loan portfolio. For example, women account for 40% of the customers of JULO in Indonesia.

3. Barriers to Women-Owned Micro, Small, and Medium-Sized Enterprises' Access to Services of Fintech Companies

Many fintechs observe significant barriers in serving WMSMEs. The main barriers are low digital and financial literacy of many WMSMEs, their lack of awareness of the availability and features of fintech services, and their inability to afford the interest charges and other fees of fintech companies.

8 RECOMMENDATIONS

Steps that can be taken by stakeholders to leverage fintech innovations to expand WMSMEs' access to finance include the following:

(1) **Need for fintech companies to collect and analyze sex-disaggregated data.** As many fintech companies do not collect gender-disaggregated data, they do not have an understanding about the size of the WMSME market or the characteristics and needs of WMSMEs.

    (a) Fintechs should implement mechanisms to measure and report on the number of women entrepreneurs they serve. This could give them an opportunity to understand the size and nature of the WMSME segment that they can serve. Such a strategy could also enable them to identify success stories of WMSME customers, which could enhance the fintech company's reputation and attract more support.

    (b) By analyzing the sex-disaggregated data, fintech companies could try to understand the needs and usage patterns of WMSMEs and use what they learn to provide more targeted lending products for WMSMEs.

(2) **Need for fintech companies to adopt a combination of online and offline processes to onboard women-owned MSMSE customers.** Because of gaps in digital and financial literacy in the case of owners of WMSMEs, offline guidance may be helpful in acquiring WMSME customers.

    (a) Fintech companies that successfully serve WMSMEs (such as Amartha in Indonesia and Growsari in the Philippines) use a combination of online and offline processes, making it easy for WMSMEs to obtain the guidance they require.

(3) **Need for stakeholders to address low digital literacy of women-owned micro, small, and medium-sized enterprises.** Addressing the lack of digital literacy of WMSMEs is important to expand the use of fintech services by WMSMEs and to truly reap financial inclusion benefits from them. Given the large number of small entities in different parts of the country who need to be reached, a wide outreach effort involving multiple stakeholders is important.

    (a) Sector-specific industry associations in sectors in which WMSMEs typically operate could coordinate achievement of this goal. For example, in Indonesia there are business associations for each sector that can be encouraged to do so,[11] such as the textile sector business association that can help organize trainings for WMSMEs in the textile business.

    (b) Financial service providers need to offer training programs that have been proven to work specifically with female segments. For example, a study in Indonesia showed that for digital financial and service platforms to build women's digital financial capabilities, financial service providers should (i) target a clear behavioral outcome and design specific methodologies, like daily SMS reminders, to help drive those changes; (ii) leverage teachable moments (e.g., with dummy apps) to help women practice their newly acquired

---

[11] Based on a virtual interview with Tulus Tambunan, professor of Indonesian economic studies and director of the Center for Industry and Small and Medium Enterprise Studies at the Faculty of Economics, University of Trisakti in Jakarta.

knowledge and abilities; and (iii) utilize social media and direct communications channels most accessible to female micro entrepreneurs (Salyanty and Askar 2022).

    (c) Central banks can play a role, as advancing financial inclusion is on their agenda and they have an overall view of the finance sector across different regions. For example, in the Philippines, the BSP has received a grant facility from Agence Française de Développement, partially for promoting digital financial literacy of rural and women-owned businesses.

(4) **Need for fintech companies to address low financial literacy of women-owned micro, small, and medium-sized enterprises.** Lack of financial literacy is one reason that WMSMEs do not feel confident approaching financiers. Financial literacy varies between regions in the same country, calling for very targeted action. In Indonesia, for example, financial literacy in rural areas was found to be 2.1% lower than that in urban areas (OJK 2022). Promoting financial literacy is a challenge because it is often neglected by finance sector participants. Below are a few examples of fintechs trying to explicitly address this issue:

    (a) KoinWorks, the Indonesian MSME-focused neobank mentioned earlier, has a learning platform in its app for financial literacy. In addition, it also conducts in-person financial literacy events. Further, it tracks the financial literacy of its users, using the OECD G20 survey on financial literacy for MSMEs as its benchmark (KoinWorks 2023).

    (b) In the Philippines, UNC Digital Bank has collaborated with Singapore-based Proxtera to promote financial literacy of MSMEs. As part of the SME Financial Empowerment Program, the collaboration seeks to train 10,000 Filipino MSMEs in financial literacy. The program offered by Proxtera, is an education program aimed to provide foundational digital financial literacy skills to SMEs. MSMEs that successfully finish the course get certified, upon which they automatically receive a UNOBank account and privileged rates of interest.

(5) **Need for stakeholders to address lack of awareness of women-owned micro, small, and medium-sized enterprises about fintech products.** One major barrier that needs to be addressed is the lack of awareness of many women microentrepreneurs about fintech initiatives.

    (a) To effectively meet the needs of WMSMEs, fintechs may need to collaborate with women's business associations or nonprofit organizations. For example, in Viet Nam, GroBanc, a fintech start-up, has created a platform for MSMEs providing a digital shopfront and e-commerce capabilities, simple tools to help them digitize and become more efficient, and access to finance. To increase awareness about the platform among WMSMEs, the start-up is working on collaborating with women's SME organizations in Ha Noi and Ho Chi Minh City.

(6) **Need for stakeholders to improve the affordability of fintech products.** As WMSMEs typically operate in low-margin businesses such as retail trade, affordability is important to ensure that the loans are viable. Because of their higher cost of funds, fintechs charge higher interest rates compared to banks, which could affect the affordability for WMSMEs. Two ways in which this issue can be addressed are a follows:

    (a) Partnerships between banks and fintech companies (in which banks provide the balance sheet for lending and fintechs provide the distribution channel for loans) could enable greater access to finance for WMSMEs at a lower cost. Moreover, fintechs use alternate data to make credit assessments instead of relying on traditional collateral and have simpler documentation requirements, addressing two important barriers that WMSMEs face with banks.

    (b) MSMEs can create a credit history with fintechs and then try to graduate to lower-cost bank finance. For example, in the Philippines, UnionBank has created an online lending marketplace, SeekCap, which caters to MSMEs nationwide. The marketplace has 15 lenders with different risk appetites to cater to MSMEs with various credit scores. On building a credit history in the marketplace, MSMEs can try to graduate to lower-cost lenders such as UnionBank.

9 CONCLUSIONS

Fintech innovations are increasingly viewed by regulators and development sector actors as part of the solution to addressing financial exclusion in developing countries. There is also recognition that fintech companies have roles that are complementary to traditional banks and that there is substantial scope for collaboration between the two. While banks have access to low cost and stable funding, their branch-based models do not allow last-mile reach and their credit assessment methodologies are unable to adequately assess the unbanked. By using data trails and technological innovations, fintech companies can make credit assessments of segments perceived to be "riskier."

WMSMEs are an important unbanked segment that can benefit from fintech innovations. Providing hard collateral is the most important barrier that WMSMEs face when accessing finance. Fintech lenders who base their credit assessments on alternate data from e-commerce, invoicing, payments, and mobile phones can enable WMSMEs to overcome this barrier. Moreover, fintechs have much simpler documentation requirements compared to traditional banks, another crucial factor in serving this segment.

The fintech sectors in Indonesia, the Philippines, and Viet Nam are well developed, though there are a few regulatory gaps in Viet Nam in some areas. While the fintech sector has developed several types of lending products that can be useful for WMSMEs, most fintechs do not focus specifically on women and, in fact, many do not track the number of women they serve. Some focus on WMSMEs because the sector they operate in is dominated by female entrepreneurs. Other than these sector-specific fintechs, there are very few examples of fintechs that intentionally tailor their products for WMSMEs.

There are several reasons why fintechs do not focus on WMSMEs. Some prefer to provide consumer loans, which is perceived to be a more lucrative market. Others believe that the universe of bankable WMSMEs is not large, even though many fintechs do not collect gender data and so are not aware of the characteristics of the WMSME segment.

Fintechs that successfully focus on low-income female entrepreneurs use a combination of online and offline processes, making it easy for WMSMEs to obtain the guidance they require. This results from a focus on building product features especially with female entrepreneurs in mind. More such initiatives are required to reach the large numbers of underserved WMSMEs. Co-lending initiatives that combine the benefits of low-cost bank lending with user-friendly fintech features would be desirable to meet WMSMEs' need for affordability and convenience. Affordability is important because WMSMEs often work in low-margin industries, while convenience is crucial as the entrepreneurs are often constrained for time because of their disproportionate share of care responsibilities.

Besides building specific products and services for WMSMEs, the barriers of low digital and financial literacy and lack of awareness about fintech products also need to be addressed to successfully serve more WMSMEs. This requires efforts from a range of stakeholders, including industry associations, central banks, fintech companies, and banks with cross-sector partnerships and collaborations.

With development finance institutions increasingly deploying more impact-oriented capital to support inclusive fintechs, there should be more opportunities for fintechs to verticalize their offerings and build customer-centric and tailor-made solutions specifically for the WMSME segment. Supporting WMSMEs can contribute to several important societal goals such as employment creation, female empowerment, and reduction in inequality. By serving more WMSMEs, digital lenders can not only expand their outreach and have higher social impact, but can also improve their loan portfolios by adding a segment known to have lower risk profiles and higher loyalty.

APPENDIX 1
STATISTICS RELATING TO INFRASTRUCTURE FOR FINTECHS

Country	Electricity Coverage	Internet Penetration	Social Media Users as a Share of the Population	Cell Phone Users as a Share of the Population	Smartphone Penetration
Indonesia	About 97%	77%	60.4%	128%	68.1%
Philippines	About 97%	73%	72.5%	72.5%	60.3%
Viet Nam	100%	73%	78.1%	158%	66.7%

fintechs = financial technology companies.
Sources: World Bank and DataReportal (accessed 29 May 2023).

APPENDIX 2
FINTECHS MENTIONED IN THE PAPER

No.	Country	Name of Fintech Company and Website	Primary Service	Legal / Regulatory Status	Year of Launch	Share of Female Customers[a]
1	Indonesia	Amartha https://amartha.com/en/	P2P platform	OJK-licensed P2P lender	2010	100%
2	Indonesia	BukuWarung https://bukuwarung.com/	Provision of bookkeeping, digital payments, and e-commerce solutions for MSMEs	Private company	2019	30%
3	Indonesia	Modalku https://modalku.co.id/	P2P platform	OJK-licensed P2P lender	2016	30% (for SME lending)
4	Indonesia	JULO https://www.julo.co.id/	Digital lending platform	OJK-licensed IT-based lending provider	2016	40%
5	Indonesia	Mapan https://mapan.id/	Digital rotating savings and credit organization	Private company	2007	100%
6	Indonesia	Fairbanc[b] https://fairbanc.app/	AI-powered working capital and payment solutions	Private company	2018	70%
7	Indonesia	Bank Jago https://www.jago.com/	Digital bank	OJK-licensed bank	1992	
8	Indonesia	Amaan https://amaan.co.id/	Digital solutions for women entrepreneurs	Private company	2021	100%

continued on next page

Appendix 2 *continued*

No.	Country	Name of Fintech Company and Website	Primary Service	Legal / Regulatory Status	Year of Launch	Share of Female Customers[a]
9	Indonesia	KoinWorks https://koinworks.com/	Digital bank	OJK-licensed P2P lender	2015	37%
10	Indonesia	Bank Neo Commerce https://www.bankneocommerce.co.id/	Digital bank	OJK-registered and supervised bank	1990	
11	Indonesia	digibank https://www.dbs.id/digibank/id/en/default.page	Digital offshoot of DBS Bank	OJK-licensed digital bank	2017	
12	Philippines	Growsari https://growsari.com/	B2B technology platform	Private company[c]	2015	85%
13	Philippines	UnionBank of the Philippines https://www.unionbankph.com/	Bank	BSP-licensed commercial bank	1968	
14	Philippines	UBX https://ubx.ph/	Bank fintech subsidiary	Private company	2019	
15	Philippines	UnionDigital Bank	Digital bank, subsidiary of UnionBank	BSP-licensed digital bank	2021	
16	Philippines	FinScore https://www.finscore.ph/	Alternate credit scoring company	Private company	2017	
17	Philippines	GCash https://www.gcash.com/	Digital wallet	Private company	2004	More than 50%
18	Philippines	Tonik Bank https://tonikbank.com/	Digital bank	BSP-licensed digital bank	2021	
17	Philippines	UNO Digital Bank https://uno.bank/	Digital bank	BSP-licensed digital bank	2021	
18	Philippines	GoTyme https://www.gotyme.com.ph/	Digital bank	BSP-licensed digital bank	2022	
19	Philippines	Cantilan Bank https://cantilanbank.com/	Rural bank	BSP-regulated rural bank	1980	
20	Philippines	First Circle https://www.firstcircle.ph/	Digital lending platform	Private company	2015	
21	Philippines	Blend.ph https://blend.ph/	P2P platform	Private company	2018	

continued on next page

Appendix 2 *continued*

No.	Country	Name of Fintech Company and Website	Primary Service	Legal / Regulatory Status	Year of Launch	Share of Female Customers[a]
22	Viet Nam[b]	Trusting Social https://trustingsocial.com/	Alternate credit scoring company	Private company	2013	
23	Viet Nam	KiotViet https://www.kiotviet.vn/	Provision of cloud-based store management software	Private company	2014	60%
24	Viet Nam	Timo Digital Bank https://timo.vn/en/	Digital bank	Private company in partnership with Viet Capital Bank, a commercial bank.	2015	
25	Viet Nam	GroBanc https://grobanc.com/	Digital platform for MSMEs	Private company	2023	
26	Viet Nam	Validus https://validus.vn/en/	P2P platform	Private company	2015	

AI = artificial intelligence; B2B = business-to-business; BSP = Bangko Sentral ng Pilipinas; IT = information technology; MSME = micro, small, and medium-sized enterprise; OJK = Financial Services Authority (Otoritas Jasa Keuangan); P2P = peer-to-peer; SME = small and medium-sized enterprise.

[a] Where available.
[b] Company is based in Singapore.
[c] The group company is an SEC licensed lending company.
[d] Owned by Mynt.

Source: Authors.

REFERENCES

Abdul Latif Jameel Poverty Action Lab. 2021. IIFI Blog Series: E-commerce Platforms as a Path to Women's Financial Inclusion. 16 December. https://www.povertyactionlab.org/blog/12-16-21/ifii-blog-series-e-commerce-platforms-path-womens-financial-inclusion.

Acclime Vietnam. 2023. Viet Nam Fintech Brief in 2023. Ho Chi Minh City. https://vietnam.acclime.com/guides/vietnam-fintech-brief-in-2023/.

AFI. 2023. A Policy Framework for Women-led MSME Access to Finance (V.2). Kuala Lumpur. https://www.afi-global.org/publications/a-policy-framework-for-women-led-msme-access-to-finance/.

Agcaoili, L. 2023. Loans to MSMEs Grow, But Still Below Threshold. *The Philippine Star*. 14 April. https://www.philstar.com/business/2023/04/14/2258685/loans-msmes-grow-still-below-threshold.

AltFi. 2020. Digital Banks are More Popular with Men. 9 December. https://www.altfi.com/article/7358_digital-banksare-more-popular-with-men.

Asian Development Bank (ADB). 2022. *Financial Instruments to Strengthen Women's Economic Resilience to Climate Change and Disaster Risks*. Manila. https://www.adb.org/publications/financial-instruments-women-economic-resilience.

Beck, T. 2020. Fintechs and Financial Inclusion: Opportunities and Pitfalls. *ADB Institute Working Paper Series*. No. 1165. Tokyo: ADB Institute. https://www.adb.org/sites/default/files/publication/623276/adbi-wp1165.pdf.

Bialus, D. et al. 2022. Financial Access of Women-Owned Small and Medium-Sized Enterprises in Viet Nam. *ADB Southeast Asia Working Paper Series*. No. 22. Manila. https://www.adb.org/sites/default/files/publication/850891/financial-access-women-owned-smes-viet-nam.pdf.

Bian, W., Cong L., and Y. Ji. 2023. The Rise of E-Wallets and Buy-Now-Pay-Later: Payment Competition, Credit Expansion, and Consumer Behavior. *National Bureau of Economic Research Working Paper*. No. 31202. https://www.nber.org/papers/w31202.

Boston Consulting Group. 2023. *Global Fintech 2023: Reimagining the Future of Finance*. https://www.bcg.com/publications/2023/future-of-fintech-and-banking.

BusinessWorld. 2023. SEC: 67% of MSMEs are Experiencing Credit Constraints. 16 February. https://www.bworldonline.com/corporate/2023/02/16/505141/sec-67-of-msmes-are-experiencing-credit-constraints/.

Canada–Indonesia Trade and Private Sector Assistance Project. 2019. *Enhancing Access to Capital for Women-Owned SMEs*. Jakarta. https://www.iccc.or.id/wp-content/uploads/2020/08/Enhancing-Access-to-Capital-for-Women-Owned-SMEs-May-2019-1.pdf.

Centennial Asia Advisors and Independent Research & Advisory Indonesia. 2018. *Why Women-Owned Businesses in Indonesia Stay Small*. http://irai.co.id/wpcontent/uploads/2018/09/Indonesia-Women-SMEs-Report-FINAL-31-Aug-18.pdf.

Centre for Impact Investing and Practices (CIIP). 2023. *Financial Inclusion in Post-COVID Southeast Asia: Accelerating Impact Beyond Access*. https://ciip.com.sg/knowledge-hub/research-insights/Details/financial-inclusion-in-postcovid-southeast-asia-accelerating-impact-beyond-access.

Chen, S. et al. 2021. The Fintech Gender Gap. *BIS Working Papers*. No. 931. Basel: Bank for International Settlements. https://www.bis.org/publ/work931.pdf.

Clawson, T. 2023. A Question of Priorities - Do Women See Entrepreneurship Differently? *Forbes*. 19 March. https://www.forbes.com/sites/trevorclawson/2023/03/19/a-question-of-prioritiesdo-women-see-entrepreneurshipdifferently/?sh=2bbc2fe0542a.

D'Espallier, B., I. Guérin, and R. Mersland. 2011. Women and Repayment in Microfinance: A Global Analysis. *World Development*. 39 (5). pp. 758–772. https://econpapers.repec.org/article/eeewdevel/v_3a39_3ay_3a2011_3ai_3a5_3ap_3a758-772.htm.

Financial Alliance for Women. 2021a. *Measuring the Value of the Female Economy: 2021 Edition*. Brooklyn. https://financialallianceforwomen.org/download/measuring-the-value-of-the-female-economy-2021-edition/.

———. 2021b. *How Fintechs Can Capture the Female Economy*. Brooklyn. https://financialallianceforwomen.org/download/how-fintechs-can-capture-the-female-economy/.

Financial Services Authority (OJK). 2022. National Financial Literacy and Inclusion Survey. https://www.ojk.go.id/iru/policy/detailpolicy/9625/press-release-2022-national-financial-literacy-and-inclusion-survey.

findexable. 2022. Global Findex Ranking 2021. https://findexable.com/ (accessed 8 August 2023).

Fintech News Philippines. 2023. All the Key Things That Happened in Philippines' Fintech Scene in Q1 2023. 31 March. https://fintechnews.ph/57890/fintechphilippines/all-the-key-things-that-happened-in-philippines-fintech-scenein-q1-2023/.

GoTyme Bank. 2023. GoTyme Bank: A Matter of Trust. 1 July 2023. https://www.gotyme.com.ph/media/stories/amatter-of-trust/.

Government of the Philippines, Department of Trade and Industry. 2022. MSME Statistics. https://www.dti.gov.ph/resources/msme-statistics/ (accessed 8 August 2023).

Government of the Philippines, Philippine Institute for Development Studies. 2023. BSP says female owned MSMEs disadvantaged in accessing capital. https://www.pids.gov.ph/details/news/in-the-news/bsp-says-female-owned-msmes-disadvantaged-in-accessing-capital.

Government of Viet Nam, Ministry of Finance. 2021. Customers Need More Understanding About Financial Servces. 31 May. https://mof.gov.vn/webcenter/portal/tttpen/pages_r/l/detail?dDocName=MOFUCM201181.

GSM Association. 2023. The Mobile Gender Gap Report 2023. London. https://www.gsma.com/r/wp-content/uploads/2023/07/The-Mobile-Gender-Gap-Report-2023.pdf.

Hoang, T. X., and C. V. Nguyen. 2022. *Men- and Women-Owned/Led MSMEs and the COVID-19 Policy Responses in Viet Nam*. https://www.monash.edu/__data/assets/pdf_file/0006/2932422/Final-country-report-MSME-gendered-impacts-Vietnam.pdf.

International Finance Corporation (IFC). 2012. *Micro, Small and Medium Enterprise Finance in India*. Washington, DC. https://www.ifc.org/en/insights-reports/2013/msme-report.

———. 2016. *Women-owned SMEs in Indonesia: A Golden Opportunity for Local Financial Institutions*. Washington, DC. https://documents1.worldbank.org/curated/en/691661477568338609/pdf/109534-WP-ENGLISH-SME-Indonesia-Final-Eng-PUBLIC.pdf.

———. 2021. Women and e-commerce in Southeast Asia. Washington, DC. https://www.ifc.org/en/insights-reports/2021/women-and-ecommerce-sea.

———. 2022a. IFC's First Investment in an NBFI in the Philippines to Support Women-owned Small Businesses, Drive Post-COVID Recovery. News release. 6 May. https://pressroom.ifc.org/all/pages/PressDetail.aspx?ID=26961.

———. 2022b. Closing the Gender Finance Gap Through the Use of Blended Finance. Washington, DC. https://www.ifc.org/en/insights-reports/2022/closing-the-gender-finance-gap-through-blended-finance.

International Labour Organization. 2018. Care Work and Care Jobs for the Future of Decent Work. https://www.ilo.org/global/topics/care-economy/old-care-for-fow/lang--en/index.htm (accessed on 11 March 2024).

Jenik, I., and P. Zetterli. 2020. *Digital Banks: How Can They Deepen Financial Inclusion?* Washington, DC: CGAP https://www.cgap.org/research/reading-deck/digital-banks-how-can-they-deepen-financial-inclusion.

Kelly, S., and M. Mirpourian. 2021. *Algorithmic Bias, Financial Inclusion, and Gender: A Primer on Opening Up New Credit to Women in Emerging Economies.* New York: Women's World Banking. https://www.womensworldbanking.org/wp-content/uploads/2021/02/2021_Algorithmic_Bias_Report.pdf.

KoinWorks. 2023. *KoinWorks Impact Report 1st Edition 2022: Leveling Up Beyond Finance.* Jakarta. https://koinworks.com/wp-content/uploads/2023/03/Impact-Report-2022_NEO-1619.pdf.

Limcaoco, P. 2021. An Embedded Finance Platform Helps Mom-and-Pop Shops Grow in Indonesia. *Accion.* 30 June. https://www.accion.org/an-embedded-finance-platform-helps-mom-and-pop-shops-grow-in-indonesia.

Manila Standard. 2022. GCash Innovations Help Boost Women-Led Enterprises in the Philippines. 31 March. https://manilastandard.net/tech/314218300/gcash-innovations-help-boost-women-led-enterprises-in-the-philippines.html.

McKinsey. 2022. Unlocking Value in Viet Nam's Banking Market for SMEs and MSMEs. 27 April. https://www.mckinsey.com/featured-insights/future-of-asia/countries-and-regions/southeast-asia/southeast-asia-perspectives/unlocking-value-in-vietnams-banking-market-for-smes-and-msmes.

Monash University, Development and Policies Research Center. n.d. *Men- and Women-Owned/Led MSMEs and the COVID-19 Policy Responses in Vietnam.* https://www.monash.edu/__data/assets/pdf_file/0006/2932422/Final-country-report-MSME-gendered-impacts-Vietnam.pdf.

Organisation for Economic Co-operation and Development (OECD). 2022a. 2022 Updated G20/OECD High Level Principles on SME Financing. Paris. https://www.oecd.org/cfe/smes/2022-Update-OECD-G20-HLP-on-SMEFinancing.pdf.

———. 2022b. Financing SMEs and Entrepreneurs 2022: An OECD Scoreboard. Paris. https://www.oecd-ilibrary.org/sites/13753156-en/index.html?itemId=/content/component/13753156-en#section-d1e148672.

Philippine Statistics Authority. 2022 Philippine MSME Statistics. https://www.dti.gov.ph/resources/msme-statistics/ (accessed 8 August 2023).

Priyono, B., G. Pancawati, and K. Ginting. 2023. The Role of Women SME's in Economic Recovery During the Covid-19 Pandemic in NTT Province. The 4th International Conference on Governance, Public Administration, and Social Science. KnE Life Sciences. pp. 543–552. https://knepublishing.com/index.php/KnE-Social/article/view/13571/21843.

Quimba, F., M. Barral, and J. Carlos. 2023. Analysis of the Fintech Landscape in the Philippines. *Research Paper Series.* No. 2023-01. Manila: Government of the Philippines, Philippine Institute for Development Studies. https://www.pids.gov.ph/publication/research-paper-series/analysis-of-the-fintech-landscape-in-the-philippines.

Rizki, K. 2022. How Digitalization is Accelerating the Growth of MSMEs in Indonesia. *World Economic Forum*. 17 May. https://www.weforum.org/agenda/2022/05/digitalization-growth-indonesia-msmes/.

Robocash Group.2022. Robocash Group: SEA-2022: State of Asian Fintech. Singapore. https://drive.google.com/file/d/1S3nRkjzy_ozg-Xb0x3qVXtTLnmFibHxP/view.

Salyanty, A., and M. Aksar. 2022. *Economic Resilience and Digital Adoption among Ultra-Micro Entrepreneurs in Indonesia*. Women's World Banking. 5 April. https://www.womensworldbanking.org/insights/report-economic-resilience-and-digital-adoption-among-ultra-micro-entrepreneurs-in-indonesia/.

Schou-Zibell, L., and S. Corley. 2022. If Carefully Managed, "Buy Now Pay Later" Can Bring More People into the Financial System. Asian Development Blog. 7 September. https://blogs.adb.org/blog/if-carefully-managed-buy-now-pay-later-can-bring-more-people-financial-system.

Schou-Zibell, L., and A. Husar. 2023. Cloud Computing Can Be a Key Enabler of Financial Inclusion. Asian Development Blog. 9 February. https://blogs.adb.org/blog/cloud-computing-can-be-key-enabler-financial-inclusion.

Sey, A. 2021. Gender Digital Equality Across ASEAN. *ERIA Discussion Paper Series*. No. 958. Economic Research Institute for ASEAN and East Asia. https://www.eria.org/publications/gender-digital-equality-across-asean/.

Shu, C. 2020. Meet BukuWarung, the Book-keeping App Built for Indonesia's 60 Million Micro Merchants. TechCrunch. 2 July. https://techcrunch.com/2020/07/02/meet-bukuwarung-the-bookkeeping-app-built-for-indonesias-60-million-micro-merchants/.

———. 2022. Fairbanc Provides BNPL for Micro-merchants in Indonesia. TechCrunch. 21 July. https://techcrunch.com/2022/07/21/fairbanc-provides-bnpl-for-micro-merchants-in-indonesia/.

State Bank of Vietnam. 2023. Enhancing Accessibility to Bank Loans for SMEs. News release. 17 March. https://www.sbv.gov.vn/webcenter/portal/en/home/sbv/news/Latestnews/Latestnews_chitiet?left-Width=20%25&-showFooter=false&showHeader=false&dDocName=SBV565014&rightWidth=0%25&center Width=80%25&_afrLoop=43467317785198466#%40%3F_afrLoop%3D43467317785198466%26center Width%3D80%2525%26dDocName%3DSBV565014%26leftWidth%3D20%2525%26rightWidth%3D0%2525%-26showFooter%3Dfalse%26showHeader%3Dfalse%26_adf.ctrl-state%3Dqucmnv6mv_9.

United Nations Development Programme, Philippines Country Office. 2020. MSME Value Chain: Rapid Response Survey (Wave 2). Mandaluyong City. https://dtiwebfiles.s3-ap-southeast-1.amazonaws.com/COVID19Resources/Reports/MSME+Value+Chain+Rapid+Response+Survey_Wave+2.pdf.

United Nations Industrial Development Organization. 2022. Outlook and Trends for Philippine MSMEs in the Evolving Business Landscape. Policy Workshop. https://sdgs.un.org/sites/default/files/2022-05/Teddy%20Monroy%2C%20UNIDO%2C%20Outlook%20and%20Trends%20for%20Philippine%20MSMEs%20in%20the%20Evolving%20Business%20Landscape.pdf.

Women Entrepreneurs Finance Initiative. 2019. Women Accelerating Vibrant Enterprises in Southeast Asia and the Pacific (WAVES) Program. Washington, DC. https://we-fi.org/wp-content/uploads/2019/02/ADB-Proposal-for-We-Fi-Funding-WAVES-Feb-14-2019.pdf.

World Bank. 2021. The Global Findex Database 2021: Financial Inclusion, Digital Payments, and Resilience in the Age of COVID-19. Washington, DC. https://www.worldbank.org/en/publication/globalfindex.

———. n.d. *Women, Business and the Law*. https://wbl.worldbank.org/en/wbl.